Happy Reading!

David A. [illegible]

A little place of poetry
With warmth on every page.
A rhyming place most notably
Made for the modern age.

A HANDFUL OF

POETRY SEEDLINGS

by David A Thornton

Printed by Book Printing UK (Peterborough)

First published in Great Britain by David's Poems
The Rhyming Corner

Printed and bound in Great Britain by Book Printing UK, Peterborough, England.

ISBN located on the back cover.

The Rhyming Corner
Wharncliffe Side
Sheffield S35 0DT

www.davidspoems.co.uk

This book is dedicated to

Cathy, Karen, Carol, Christine, Jill, Patricia, Alizon, Mavis, Margaret, Sandie, Andrew, Sally, Elaine, Janice, Frances, Mary, Carolyne, Sylvie, Eleanor, Millie, Rupert, Janet, Shona, Rosie, Margery, Mal, Brenda, Alice, Barbara, Maggie, Bev, Yvonne, Jayne, Peter, Davina, Patty, Elsie, Hilary, Michael, Bex, Steve, Pauline, Sharron, Elizabeth, Vanessa, Joyce, Helena, Marilyn, Kathy, Brenda, Jane, Valerie, Eileen, Angela, Linda, Jess, Jackie, Nicky, Mark, Molly, Mave, Dorothy, Jean, Susan, Sophie, Andy, Celia, Gill, Kate, Anne, Kay, Val, Amanda, Ann, Tanya, Wilma, Marion, Dave, Brett, Caroline, Julie, Sandra, June, Doreen, Denise, Joan, Marie, Lily, Beryl, Rita, Cath, Gina, Bernie, Eric, Adonis and Jo.

And all my other Facebook friends who kept me going this year.

Thank You.

Contents

Introduction

My grandma lived in Burley in Wharfedale, which seemed like an awfully long way from Sheffield when I was six years old. We would visit her a few times every year in our family car, a grey VW beetle which bore the number plate WOO 2OO.

Car journeys across the moors were always full of anticipation, as a visit to grandma's house meant presents, lemonade, and a colour telly. We didn't have a colour TV in those days, although my friend had one you could fix a striped coloured plastic screen over the front of. It sounds like a totally daft idea these days, and indeed it was. The plastic screen was divided into three colours, blue across the top for the sky, green across the bottom for the grass, and a sort of reddish tint in the middle. It was the closest we could get to colour TV in the late sixties, unless we were going to grandma's house.

My dad was not known for his patience, especially when driving, and it was not unusual for some minor catastrophe to occur en route. Once the gears stuck and we had to crawl the whole way back in second with a tailback of angry traffic scowling at us all through the centre of Huddersfield.

Another time the engine, which was in the boot, decided to challenge my pipe smoking father to see who could produce the most obnoxious fumes during a single car journey. The VW won, just.

Nevertheless, we loved going to grandma's house, and as the big day approached we would gather together items we wanted to bring along. For my five year old sister this was her floppity rabbit, and for me it was my treasured Rupert Bear annuals.

I was infatuated with Rupert Bear. His adventures made all the more graphic thanks to the wonderful illustrations carefully drawn by Alfred Bestall, but it was the words that really got me. Rupert Bear stories were laid out with two lines of rhyming verse under each illustration, and although there was also a paragraph of descriptive text running across the bottom of the page, I never bothered reading those.

It was the simplicity of the rhyme, and the comfort of the satisfying cadences that made these Christmas annuals such a pleasure to read. I would scan the picture above, adding context, more detail and perhaps even starting to fill in other parts of the story that were not directly indicated by the rhyming couplet set out below.

At some point, and I can't remember exactly when, I started to make up my own rhyming adventures. These often rather gruesome little tales were usually designed to distract, entertain and sometimes terrify my little sister whilst rumbling through the moors in our smokey little car.

Years later, whilst clearing out my mum's basement, following a decision that it was time for her to downsize, I came across my pile of Rupert annuals. They were rather dusty, a little damp, and packed with felt tip annotations and additional illustrations penned by me almost fifty years earlier.

Something clicked. Over the next few years I went from the occasional reader of poetry to a massive consumer, I devoured everything from Sylvia Plath to Pam Ayres, Sophocles to John Betjeman, Shakespeare to the War Poets, and inevitably I began to play around with verse myself.

Whilst I enjoy most poetry, it is simple accessible rhymes that entertain and satisfy me the most. I think I'm probably still writing to distract people from challenging journeys. My sincere hope is that these little poetry seedlings will put a smile on your face and perhaps take you on the odd adventure just like those Rupert Bear annuals did for me all those years ago.

David A Thornton
November 2020

www.davidspoems.co.uk

Being Here

Racing blindly round the bend,
Jumping forward to the end,
Skimming over boring text,
Chasing after what comes next.

The fresh allure of pastures new,
Promising a better view,
The greener grass, not far away,
Inviting us to come and stay.

We never look before we leap,
And often jump in way too deep,
Fast-forwarding to what comes next,
Missing out on life's subtext.

Life shouldn't be a constant race,
Let's vote today for slower pace,
And take some time to figure out,
What being here is all about.

Climbing Trees

Scruffed up trousers, dirty knees,
Today we're outside climbing trees.
Ancient oaks on the village green
And Sycamores by the old mill stream.
Tall and strong, these sky-stairs stand
Proud old watchers on the land,
Nodding slightly in the breeze
"come and climb up if you please".
The hardest part is getting going,
Finding footholds, slipping, slowing
Faces press against the bark,
Hugging tree trunks in the park.
And then we reach the lower boughs
With dripping sweat upon our brows,
Here we rest, take in the view,
And climb on up, refreshed anew.
Higher, higher, don't look down!
But straight ahead, to the distant town
Or out to sea and the fishing boats,
With sailors in their overcoats.

This hallowed place, here in the tree
Just me, the air, the land, the sea.

So after sitting still for hours,
It's time to climb down these watchtowers,
Slow at first, then in a rush,
We slide, then skid, our faces blush.
The world above is in retreat
And then we're back upon on our feet.
The world around looks different now,
My viewpoint has been changed somehow,

You're never quite the same you see,
Once you climb down from a tree.

Stormageddon

A nightmare crashed into our town,
And tore all of the houses down,
Stormforce ten or ten point five
Will anyone be left alive?

A hoarding just blew down the street,
And knocked the news crew off their feet,
It's like some classic movie scene,
Surreal, a dream, not real I mean.

A lorry slides across the road,
The petrol station will explode.
Bits of trees fly through the air,
A washing line, some underwear.

People run for basement safety,
Despite foundations looking shaky,
Some are fleeing in their cars,
Whilst others hide in downtown bars.

Then nothing. Everything goes still,
No one moves, or breathes, until
We know the worst of it has gone
And peace returns,
And life moves on.

That Lightbulb Moment

Ever had a lightbulb moment?
Everything goes clear.
Then suddenly, within your head,
You get a great idea.

There you are, just standing still,
Then like a bolt of lightning,
A tiny spark ignites your brain,
Ka-boom! with perfect timing.

Sometimes though, the light plays tricks,
You think you're innovating,
Then find that someone got there first,
And that is so frustrating!

A February Morning on the Beach

We must go to the beach today,
Let's walk along the prom,
In coats and gloves, and bobble hats,
To see what's going on.

The kiosks are still boarded up,
The season's not begun,
Eastern winds swirl round the bay,
No warmth yet in the sun.

And yet, it's busy on the front,
Easter, weeks away,
Painters, builders, salesmen, cleaners,
"Lots to do" they say

Deliveries are coming in,
To fill the sea front stores,
The deckchair man is painting stripes,
On twenty beach hut doors.

Café owners buy their stock,
Of giant coffee tins,
Whilst Council workers on the path,
Are cleaning litter bins.

The theatre puts a poster up,
To sell the summer shows,
The Pier erects a brand new sign
“Open soon” it glows.

Everyone's excited here,
The season is approaching,
“This year”, they say, “will be our best”,
At least that's what they're hoping.

We sit and watch these busy folk,
We're lucky living here,
To see the seaside waking up
and start another year.

Natural High

We went to find the big outdoors,
A plan we'd had for weeks,
To head off on a great escape,
And climb the highest peaks.

Our rucksacks were so heavy,
With coats piled up on top,
Woolly hats and picnic mats,
And drinks for when we'd stop.

First we cross the stepping stones,
Squelching in the clay,
Wearing hoods, then through the woods,
We were on our way.

We climbed up through a steep ravine,
Our legs were feeling weak,
Past the mill, then higher still,
We climbed towards the peak.

And as we reached the very top,
Relieved that we were there,
Nothing else above us,
Surrounded by the air.

The city was a distant speck,
A million miles away,
All the World below us,
We were mountain kings that day.

And In that moment, on the peak,
Neither of us had to speak,
For on that mountain in the sky,
We had found our Natural High

The Body Politic

The Body woke this morning
And Hand said to The Brain,
“I've had enough of being here
I'd rather not remain”.

The Arms then both went crazy,
Folded in disgust,
They fell out with each other,
The Body lost all trust.

The Brain called an election,
The result was such a riddle,
Half will go, half will stay,
Cut right down the middle!

Eyes would not look at The Ears,
And let their eyelids close,
The Head became a sticky mess,
No Hands to blow its nose.

The Shoulders were unhappy,
Carrying that weight,
Tummy kept on grumbling,
And Ears could not relate.

Hands refused to work with Legs,
Knees refused to bend,
The Body was in turmoil, and just
Lay there in the end.

The moral of this sordid tale,
Is recognise you're part
Of a bigger situation,
And respect that from the start.

The Top of Everything

"What goes up, must then come down"
But what if that's not true?
You might just keep on going up and that is all you do.
At first it feels quite clever, floating in the air,
Your feet rise off the pavement with nothing under there.

Up above the houses, and past the tops of trees,
Everything is shrinking, when I look down past my knees.
I'm floating past an office block, hello ninetieth floor!
A bird flew past, and almost died of shock at what he saw.

Up I go, on into clouds, where it starts to rain,
I just waved at the people in a passing Jumbo plane.
Now it's getting darker, this must be the stratosphere.
I should have brought a space suit to come flying right up here.

I think I saw a Martian, in a rocket, close to Mars,
I had to make a detour not to crash into the stars,
Now the sky is milky, with swirls just like ice cream,
The Universe gets smaller still, until it can't be seen.

But now it's getting brighter, with a glow that's all around,
I've reached the top of everything, furthest from the ground.
My head bobs gently on the roof, my feet just hanging there.
I get the sense that I've arrived, this seems to be somewhere.

I suppose I am quite tired; I could do with a rest,
Perhaps a comfy pillow, and a long sleep would be best.

I've had a good long innings,
I've got nothing left to fear,
And yes, I'll miss my loved ones,
But I'll watch them from up here.

Forever Young

On the occasion of Bob Dylan's birthday
24th May

Bob Dylan, he was born today,
In nineteen forty one,
A poet and a troubadour
Bettered yet by none.

Whether blowing in the wind,
Or tangled up in blue,
His thoughtful lyrics strike a chord,
His message fresh and new.

Though times may now be changing,
He remains a rolling stone
Not meant for the establishment
He walks his path alone.

He may not stay forever young,
And hard rain may well fall,
But happy birthday to you Bob,
Your songs have touched us all.

The Boxer

A Box, this is my cardboard box,
But also it's my World,
A wishing well, or posh hotel,
In which you'll find me curled.

It's large enough to sit in,
And imagine you're at sea,
Or trekking through the Amazon,
It means so much to me.

It's brown and corrugated,
Like the roof on dad's old shed,
Cosy in the winter nights,
In sunshine cool instead.

My box is full of hopes and dreams,
Better times will come,
A place where I can hide away,
From almost anyone.

I really like my cardboard box,
I keep it clean and neat,
I haven't got another home,
As I live on the street.

Lighthouse Family

Fair weather friends,
where are you now,
has rain washed you away?
So much for all
those welcome smiles,
is all that I can say.

Life can get uncomfortable,
and storms can rage around,
but friends, they are an anchor,
and a fog horn warning sound.

So when your ship hits stormy seas,
and you need my support,
I'll still be here,
And have no fear,
I'll help you in to port.

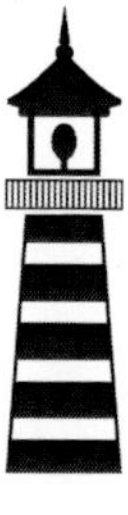

When I am Old

When I am old,
I will be bold,
I'll do my exercise.
I may resist,
But will persist,
To keep me mobilised.

I will sing,
All morning,
And dance all afternoon,
Then I'll walk,
Or sit and talk,
Or 'face-tube' in my room.

I'll keep my mind,
Bright and kind,
And not dress like a frump,
But mostly I,
Will just get by,
And not become a grump.

Later

Later, you traitor,
You always delay,
Fine 'till tomorrow,
Is all you can say.

Later says wait,
Let's not do this yet,
Best to postpone,
Perhaps to forget.

Buy now pay later,
No need for distress,
Get all you want,
Without all of the stress.

Later looks lovely,
Free from all pains,
Put offs are gorgeous,
For hope still remains.

But sooner or later,
We have to take chances,
And live for the moment,
To make our advances.

Instant Fix

Convenience, you temptress,
Driven by the clocks.
The lure of something instant,
Straight out of a box.

Life-style show contestants,
Winning instant fame,
And quick-fix renovators
Who cover up their game.

Transformation stories,
The folklore of our days,
Promising to change our lives,
In rapid easy ways.

Breaking news across the globe,
Updates every hour,
Social comment by live feed,
Instant super power.

Can we take a moment
To stop and watch things grow?
Let's take the World more slowly
And not miss half the show.

Battlefield to Butterflies

The battlefields of World War One,
A shell-shocked no man's land,
Where death walked through the trenches,
And took each soldiers hand.

A battered, shattered, hostile land,
Of sorrow, pain and fear,
And prayers that soon the war would end,
Perhaps by Spring next year.

Then in this muddy battlefield,
A butterfly appears,
Wings of white, with bright red tips,
Like blood, wept through the years.

It flits across the British trenches,
Over no man's land,
And rests upon a Gatling gun,
Close to a German's hand.

The soldier pauses for a while,
To gaze upon this sight,
This fragile beauty fills his heart,
With joy far from the fight.

And now so many years have passed,
In time the land has healed,
For seeds of peace have been released,
Across the battlefield.

Poppies grow where blood was shed,
And dance against blue skies,
Now nature's forces are deployed,
One million butterflies.

The Actor Prepares

Real and unreal,

Technical star,

Line learning hypocrite,

Truth in a jar.

Deviant lover,

Strutter of dreams,

Beggars belief,

Not what he seems.

Hero most noble,

Darkling desires,

A child on the shoulders

Of tricksters and liars.

Goooaaaal!

That magic feeling,
When he slams it in the net,
The opposition reeling,
His best performance yet.

Schooled in fancy footwork,
Rather than exams,
No aptitude for bookwork,
But full of massive plans.

"You never will amount to much"
They used to say in class,
And yet he had the golden touch,
In playgrounds or on grass.

From back streets to the stadium,
A jedi with the ball,
I guess it turned out that he had
The best results of all.

Bedtime

I know just what you're thinking,
It can't be bedtime yet,
But actually, as you can see,
It is. Get over it.

Snuggle down, get comfy,
Is your pillow straight?
Have you left your socks on?
Come on, it's getting late.

Let's drift off to the land of nod,
Although it sounds quite boring,
Not a place to party at,
With everyone just snoring.

And actually "The Sandman",
Always worried me a bit,
I preferred Peter Pan,
Now I think of it.

Either way, I have to say,

You need go to sleep,

Please ignore my ramblings,

Forget this Sandman creep.

You want to have a story?

Well, I'm reading you this rhyme,

Tomorrow maybe, if you're good,

Now have you seen the time?

Close your eyes, make flutterbys,

Practise some more yawning.

Pleasant dreams my special one,

and see you in the morning.

Alfred's Adventures

Alfred was a Polar Bear,
Who lived on Arctic ice,
And liked to spend his evenings
Underneath the Northern Lights.

One night whilst he was snoozing,
After quite a day,
The ice sheet he was sleeping on,
Snapped and broke away.

Poor Alfred didn't know it,
For he was fast asleep,
But on he floated through the night,
Above the oceans deep.

At last Alfred was woken,
By the sunshine in his eyes,
He raised a lazy eyelid,
Then stood up in surprise.

He could see a palm tree,
On a beach of golden sand,
And a group of complete strangers
All with iphones in their hand.

Yes, they made him welcome,
It was nice to feel the sun,
He learnt to surf out on the sea,
And had a lot of fun.

But soon, he missed his snowy home,
He longed to be back there.
At times he thought, this isn't me,
I am a Polar Bear.

Next day when Nordic Cruises,
Sailed into the bay,
Alfred took his chance and he
Became a stow-a-way.

He had to stay well-hidden
For twenty days and nights,
But then he heard the captain say
"Behold, the Northern lights!"

Alfred leapt up full of joy,
He raced off on his own,
It was good to have adventures,
But much nicer to be home.

The Fire and the Frying Pan

When man discovered fire,
Or woman, (either one),
It must have been fantastic
To share what they had done.

Lighting up the caves at night,
Heating up a pot,
But soon they saw the downside,
Flames are dangerously hot.

The burning issue of the day was
Light your fire with care!
In modern times, we understand,
We're "fire-safe aware".

Then we discovered plastic,
Which does fantastic things,
But now we've come to realise
The damage that it brings.

Use it once, it stays around,
Floating in our seas,
Is it in our food chain now?
There are no guarantees.

Plastic was quite useful,
And did impressive stuff,
But honestly, It seems to me
The Earth has had enough.

Just like fire, treat with care,
Cut out what you can.
I fear we'll leap out of the fire,
Into the frying pan.

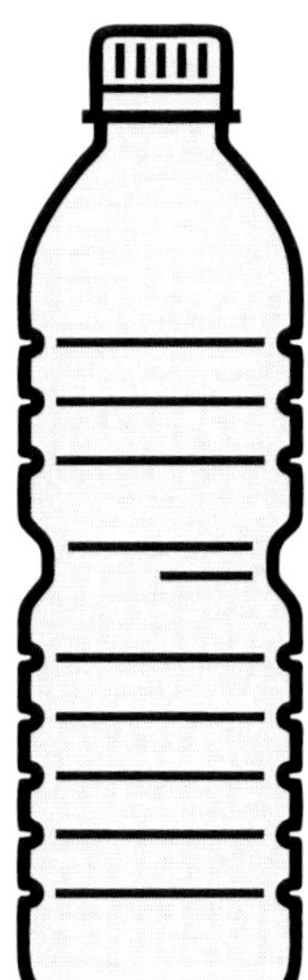

The Dragon's Toothache

A dragon with a toothache,
Is a most alarming sight,
Especially if he has to go to
Battle with a Knight

A jousting Knight had challenged him,
And caught him with his lance,
Then galloped off in victory,
Without a second glance.

So now poor dragon sits alone,
Sobbing in his claws,
"I need to get this sore tooth out"
And rubs his swollen jaws.

He puts a chain around his tooth,
Then takes the other end,
And wraps it round a boulder,
Up a mountain, round the bend.

Soon the rock begins to roll,
Yank! The chain goes tight,
The tooth flies out, and through the air,
Then whizzes out of sight.

A dragon's tooth is worth a bit,
With hidden magic powers,
Even after being rolled
Around a hill for hours.

So out on your adventures,
In the countryside this year,
Look out for that dragon's tooth,
It may be very near.

And as for our poor dragon,
He has long since flown away,
To try and find a dentist,
And to fix his tooth decay.

All those sweet young maidens!
Well, he should have brushed his teeth,
His smile has now been ruined,
By a big gap underneath.

England in Miniature

Have you ever been
To the Isle of Wight?
We went over Tuesday,
And stayed till Friday night.

Although it isn't very big,
It's larger than it looks,
And worth a bit of planning,
With your trusted travel books.

The roads are often narrow,
And they weave around a lot,
I guarantee, you'll be amazed,
At what a lot it's got.

I wouldn't like to pick one thing,
And state it as the best,
But rather say, head there today,
And put it to the test.

You have to get a ferry,

But it isn't very far,

The buses there are really good,

So no need for the car.

But if I may just recommend,

A favourite place of mine,

Godshill Model Village,

If you find you have the time

I Want Doesn't Get

I want to have an ipad,
I really really do.
Mummy's got one, it's not fair,
I need to have one too.

It's not like they're expensive,
And think of how I'll use it,
I'll make at least a million pounds,
Go on let me choose it.

Are you saying I can't have one?
That is very mean,
Buy me one this minute,
Or I'll scream and scream and scream.

Look, let's all be reasonable,
I've got some pocket money,
I'll do the dishes for a week,
Just get me one please mummy.

I didn't really want one,
I want a horse instead,
If Daddy doesn't get me one,
I might as well be dead.

I'll settle for a pony,
And a saddle and a hat,
Perhaps I need a stable too,
Now go, just get me that!

Thinking more about it,
I want to have a car,
I know I cannot drive it yet,
But mummy, be a star?

It has to be a shiny one,
It better be brand new
'Cos when I get my ipad
I'll need wifi in there too.

My Superhero Mum

I know a magic Mummy,
Who has super human skills,
She's a real Wonder Woman,
Or a Batman, but with frills.

She flies about the place all day,
And never rests at night,
No one else can beat her,
When she's breaking up a fight.

She has a way of seeing you,
With her X ray eyes,
And knowing when you tell the truth,
Or when you're telling lies.

She's always there to win with love,
Defender of your pride,
She's totally invincible,
And always by your side.

But most of all, when things get tough,
She'll rebuild half the World,
And never run away from you,
As life around you swirls.

I'm thankful for the magic,
For everything she's done,
And every time she's saved my skin,
My Superhero Mum!

Why are we here?

"Why are we here?"
asked the bright little girl,
"what is the meaning of life?"
The man thought for a moment,
and raised an eyebrow,
then turned, and looked at his wife.

"You're here thanks to love",
said the lady to her,
"and your life will be what you make".
"But WHY am I here",
insisted the girl,
"what's my PURPOSE for goodness sake?"

"There is not a point,
not a reason as such,
you take life and use it your way.
You will decide,
how you want to abide,
and how you will live every day".

"If you want our advice",
she said, being nice,
"I suggest that you live through your heart.
Be clever, be kind,
make the most of your mind,
that sounds like a great place to start".

World Photography Day

Snap! I think I've got it,
It's World photography day,
But when I saw the picture
My thumb was in the way.

You'll have to take my word for it,
It was a cracking scene
But now I just have pictures
Of where my thumb has been.

Let's Visit England

Oh, let's visit England,
To have tea, and scones and jams,
That lush inviting countryside,
Those cows, and sheep and lambs.

The wild and rugged coastline,
With hidden coves and bays,
Golden sands, and ice cream stands,
And warmer summer days.

Cities old as time itself,
With ancient city walls,
Newly covered in plate glass,
With funky bars and stalls.

Paths for walking by the sea,
Or through the hills and dales,
Cycle Paths, and Roman baths,
And January Sales.

And then we'll head to London Town,
To try and spot the Queen,
Then maybe try the London Eye,
And dine out in between.

Those castles, gardens, stately homes,
Well, I'm your biggest fan.
There's nowhere quite like England now,
Let's visit whilst we can!

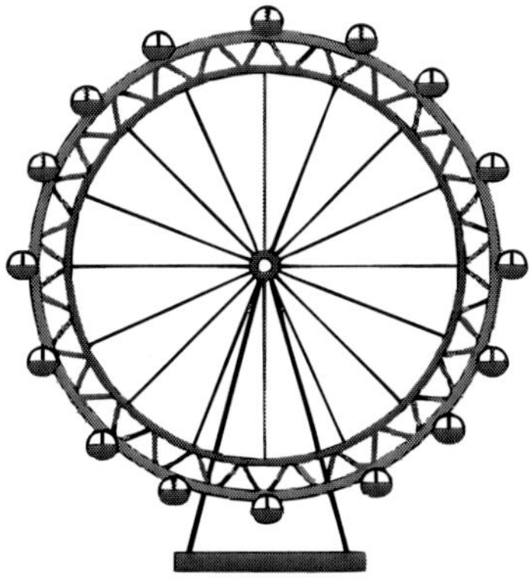

Hello Mr Sunshine!

The Sun gets up each morning,
And climbs into the sky.
He heads to bed each evening,
As the Moon comes floating by.

And so it is, and always was,
Until one fateful day,
When the Sun got up one morning,
And the Moon was in the way.

"Excuse me", said the Sunshine,
In a friendly kind of chat,
"I hate to say, you're in my way,
You know, we can't have that".

"Look here Mr Sunshine",
The Moon began to say,
"I've got the right to be here,
every single day".

"Well that just cannot happen!"
Said the Sun, now quite alarmed,
"We can't just whizz around the sky,
Someone will get harmed".

"I go first" began the Moon,
"No, me" replied the Sun,
And pretty soon a fight broke out,
Upsetting everyone.

The Sun and Moon refused to shine,
And both went skulking off,
The land plunged into darkness,
Summertime was off.

After almost seven weeks,
Folk had seen enough,
"The Sun and Moon must both be friends
It's time that we got tough".

The Sun was told he must invite,
The Moon round for her tea,
The Moon was told to thank him for
His pleasant company.

It started well, or not too bad,
But shouting soon broke out,
The Moon got rather angry,
Throwing stardust all about.

The Sun got red and flustered,
And really rather hot,
He stamped on Mars a few times,
Whilst swearing quite a lot.

"Look we need a plan" they said,
Once they both sat down,
"Can we both just start together,
Follow each around?".

"Like a sort of relay?"
Asked the Moon, in careful tone.
"We'd both set off together,
But from a different Zone?"

The Sun said "*Even better,*
We can both keep on the move,
You know, I didn't think of that,
What a team we'll prove".

And so it is, and always was,
The Sun wakes in the East,
The Moon sleeps after sailing West,
To keep the peace at least.

Looking for George

Bingo's in a Beatles band,
In fact he plays the drums,
He's always got a pair of sticks,
Resting on his thumbs.

Lennox plays the Lennon role,
He likes to play the fool,
But also plays harmonica,
On songs like "Love me Do"

Lizzie plays the bass guitar,
She sings like Paul McCartney,
And even though she's not a bloke,
She knows just how to party.

They haven't got a George right now,
The last one just got bored,
The only songs he got to sing were
"Chains" and "My Sweet Lord"

My Bin is not a Number

My bin has a new number,
It wasn't there before,
It's down to our new neighbours,
Who moved in right next door.

My bin don't want no number,
It's downcast, and depressed,
It doesn't really want to feel
A bin like all the rest.

They stuck that number on him,
without checking first you see,
It's like they're sort of saying
Don't mix your bins with me.

My bin is so brow beaten,
Labelled number 2,
And all the world now knows it,
'Cos it's stuck on there with glue.

Old Muso

Old Muso, now you're older,
Does your guitar arm get cramp?
Are nerve ends numb and colder,
When you lift up your new amp?

Have you noticed, in your voice,
A slight disturbing wobble?
And are you finding packing up
A little too much trouble?

Have all those constant set-ups
Been repeating like a wheel?
Have the late night parties
Lost their rampant sex appeal?

Do you sometimes lose your place,
Half way through a song?
And have you ever noticed that you
Play the third chord wrong?

Old Muso, you are older,
But your pulse will always beat,
To the sound you make upon the stage,
Until the song's complete.

9am on the Beach

The roar of the waves,
As they break on the beach,
Not yet drowned out,
By the clatter and screech,
Of girls in bikinis,
In Instagram poses,
And dads rubbing sun cream
On foreheads and noses.
A sunbow of parasols,
Will be displayed,
As lots of hot bodies,
Set up in the shade.
The sand freshly raked,
And the sun loungers neat,
Waiting for tourists
To put up their feet.
Oh the peace on the beach,
At the start of the day,
Before all the tourists
Get in the way.

The Easter Walk

Easter, that means 'Easter Walks'
in the pouring rain,
no matter what the weather says,
every year's the same.
Yesterday was sunny,
not a cloud in view,
but now it's thunder, lightning, rain,
with fog and strong winds too.

You'd think that we would cancel it
but mum and dad say "NO!"
We pack our lunches, extra socks,
and Easter eggs and go.
We drive into the countryside,
to some deserted spot,
with mountains all around us,
the land that time forgot.

Lunch is eaten by a wall
that feels like the North Pole,
the rain keeps beating on my head,
and on my sausage roll.

Halfway up the mountain side,
my sister needs a wee,
dad shouts out from up ahead,
"Go behind a tree".

Little sister gets her foot stuck
in a rabbit hole,
then trips and falls into the stream,
soaked from head to toe.
"Good one sis" I say to her,
"now can we all go home?"
But dad says, "race you to the top",
and sets off all alone.

Now we're walking in thick mist,
and then it starts to snow,
my dad appears to look confused,
not sure which way to go.
"Oh No, we're going to die up here",
I kick up quite a stink,
"Be quiet now", my mother says,
"and let your father think".

"I think I see a light ahead",
dad whispers in the dark,

Turns out it's a mini bus,
we're back in the car park.

Eventually we make it home,
half dead on our legs,
we sit beside a roaring fire
and eat our Easter eggs.

I wasn't always happy
on those soggy walking days,
but now, when I think back on them,
they were great holidays.

Inside Out

There was a boy with skin so blue,
As blue as sunny sky,
He turned up in our village,
And startled passers-by.

They'd not seen someone with blue skin,
Unsure of what to think,
He's not like us, they whispered,
We're used to brown and pink.

He had a truly awful time
At the local school,
People called him ‘smurf-face’,
And thought him most uncool.

Every night he cried at home,
And hated going out,
He did not feel secure at all,
When he walked about.

But then a kindly teacher,
A certain Mr Quinn,
Started asking questions,
About his coloured skin.

Tell me why it matters?
He asked the local folk,
Just because he's different,
You treat him like a joke.

You villagers have problems,
You can't see past his face,
He's still a human being,
Your reaction's a disgrace.

A wiser person judges people,
From the inside out,
Start by looking at their heart,
To see what they're about.

You must not judge a person
Just because they're blue,
It's what's inside that really counts,
That should mean more to you.

A person may be pure and kind,
Or rotten to the core,
But you just can't judge a person,
By their colour any more.

Listen!

The candle that burns brightest,
Burns down before the rest,

The car that's always speeding,
Will crash before the best.

A rocket will not reach the moon,
If no one adds the fuel,

And children who don't listen,
Will not do well at school.

One Word

We are a world of words,
That spark, and tame and frame,
Soothing sounds, some out of bounds,
Invented for the game.

A world that oft is foggy,
And filled with dark half-lies,
Fuelling our suspicions,
Appearing in disguise.

Yet words can move a mountain,
Or build bridges over streams,
And bring us all together,
As we line up into teams.

Words are ammunition,
Cannons, on front lines,
But also they're the pathways,
That calm chaotic minds.

Words can be so brutal,
Spoken for effect,
But in the end, the final word,
Is always show respect.

The Wonders of Wight

I saw it on a tea towel,
Many years ago,
The seven wonders of the Wight,
It made us want to go.

Cows you couldn't milk, was one,
(Though some have had a go),
Being dry in Lake's no fun,
With needles that can't sew.

It got me sort of thinking,
Could this be updated?
What wonders would you choose today,
And how would they be rated?

Red squirrels would be on my list,
And so would sunshine hours,
Perfect bays for Instagram,
A Garden Isle of flowers.

It is a real Adventure Land,
Where stories start to form,
Of wishing stones and pirate bones,
Where dinosaurs were born.

It has to be the countryside,
That rolls down to the sea,
Or the stately home of poets
In Freshwater Bay for me.

So when I come to 'cross the bar',
Returning to this space,
I doubt, just like Lord Tennyson,
I'd find a nicer place.

The River Cycle

Above the highest mountain
the storm clouds all are spent,
the raindrops gather in the lake
to start their long descent.

The waters reach their tipping point,
they're off! They are released,
pouring down the mountain side
the power now unleashed.

Rocks are tossed out of the way.
to form a river bed,
racing ever downwards
as the edges start to spread.

They pour into the villages,
and lap against our walls,
jumping over stepping stones,
creating waterfalls.

Resting in the village pond,
half way through the race,
warming in the sunshine
before picking up the pace.

Flowing through a lovely view
some water creeps away,
captured by the reservoirs,
saved for another day.

But then, at last, a coastal scene,
the sea within their reach,
they dive under the promenade,
and head off down the beach.

And here the river meets the sea,
but no rest for the rain,
the clouds soak up the water drops
to start off once again.

Pussykins the Spy Cat

Pussykins the spy cat,
Was not like any other,
She spent her time, fighting crime,
And often undercover.

She sometimes wore false whiskers,
Or changed her coat to white,
But mostly she had snowy paws,
With fur as black as night.

Her missions sent her round the world,
To dangerous locations,
She kept a range of pet passports,
For use in different nations.

Pussykins the spy cat,
Often worked for the Prime Minister,
On foreign shores, and on all paws,
Anything that looked sinister.

Some say she liked her morning milk,
Shaken but not stirred,
And kept her claws razor sharp,
In case you hadn't heard.

You'd find her often sitting,
On the top of some old fence,
Looking like she's half asleep
But that is just pretence.

She was watching mouse manoeuvres,
Or signalling her base,
Getting new instructions,
For her next exciting case.

It was said she had at least nine lives,
But eight had been and gone,
Yet Pussykins was sharp as knives,
And knew just when to run.

Her secret base, I shan't reveal,
I've promised not to say,
But If the country needs her back,
She will return one day.

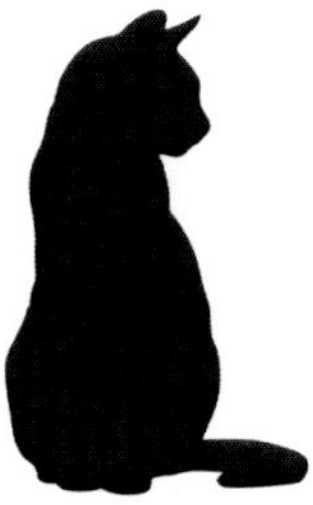

Our Day at the Zoo

What a smashing day we had,
We all went to the zoo!
Grandad dropped his false teeth
In a pile of zebra poo.

Uncle Harry's camera phone
Was new and really funky,
But then he went and let it get
Stolen by a monkey.

Harry was beside himself,
His face was red with rage,
So the monkey put the picture
On our family Facebook page.

Over in the reptile house,
Gran was feeling queasy,
A snake slid up and winked at her
And made her feel uneasy.

Daddy sat down for a while,
He said he needed rest,
A spider came and bit his arm,
For sitting on her nest.

We went to see the penguins,
Swimming round their pool,
Daisy went and jumped straight in,
So I jumped in there too.

We really liked the zoo that day,
I want to go back there,
But mummy says we're banned for life
Which I don't think is fair!

The Case of The Whitehall Mews

"Stolen Secret Papers",
Shrieked the Secretary of State,
"Call Pussykins the Spy Cat,
We've a cat to activate".

She was curled up in a chair,
Recalling, in her mind,
The time she thwarted Golden Paws,
Saving Feline Kind.

"Look" said the Prime Minister,
"We don't care what it costs,
Just get those secret papers back,
Or everything is lost".

First she flew to Russia,
To meet The Moscow Cat,
Soft me-ows to passing cows,
And other stuff like that.

She went 1st class to old Bagdad,
And saw an Arab King.
In Rome she chilled out with the Pope,
But that revealed nothing.

Then back in London one dark night,
A chase through parliament,
She forced a Whitehall cat to say,
He'd done it, and repent.

The Government was most relieved,
To have their secrets back,
And PK got her own reward,
A prawn and salmon snack.

A spy cat's job is pretty tough,
But always turns out fine,
So Pussykins can now relax,
Until that is, next time.

National Walking Month

I hear it's National Walking Month,
So best foot forward now!
It doesn't matter where you go,
Just set off anyhow.

A little shuffle, or a stride,
A jog, or just a crawl,
Go walking in the sun or rain,
It's healthy for us all.

You see so many things on foot,
That we would surely miss,
So slip your walking shoes on now,
Straight after reading this.

Walking is the kind of thing,
That we should do each day,
About a mile, performed in style,
Is best I've heard them say.

Of course you may be one of those,
Who likes an epic walk,
From Land's End up to John O'Groats,
Whilst others sit and talk.

Circular or in a line,
Or to a village inn,
It really doesn't matter much,
Just start,
Make tracks,
BEGIN.

Pictures in the Sky

If we all turn off the lights,
What then will we see?
Just a load of darkness
Staring back at me?

No! A million, zillion stars,
Are shining in the skies,
Can you see the shapes they form
By drawing with your eyes?

Did you spot Orion's Belt?
Now try and draw your own,
A unicorn, a hunter's horn,
Perhaps a large trombone?

First you focus on the stars,
And then the space between,
So in the corner of your eye,
The pictures can be seen.

Your mind will then fill in the blanks,
And soon you'll recognise,
A hidden shape, or path, or word,
And send it to your eyes.

Paint your pictures in the sky,
And you will surely be,
A person who has big ideas,
And draws them carefully.

Royal Wedding Day

Today is "Royal Wedding Day",
Thank goodness for sun,
It wouldn't feel the same at all,
With rain on everyone.

Windsor Castle gleaming bright
Starring in the news,
The whole town rocks with well -wishers,
Police and TV crews.

And then the guests start to arrive,
The crowds begin to cheer,
The Queen waves as she travels past,
She looks pleased to be here.

Everyone has tales to tell,
Of how they know the Prince,
Or when they met Ms Markle,
And how she's acted since.

And now the heart of everything,
The ceremony's here,
Everybody holds their breath,
And suddenly it's clear...

For all the trappings, all the fizz,
And all that's going on,
Actual it's just two hearts,
Who want to live as one.

Lovers, be they Kings or serfs,
They make our world go round,
So everyone who is in love,
Today should all be crowned.

Written on the occasion of the wedding between
Prince Harry and Megan Markle on the 19th of May
2018

Invasion!

One dark and stormy Thursday,
In the middle of the night,
I was woken early,
By a strong pulsating light.

A space rocket had landed,
In the back, behind our shed,
Some robot with a booster gun
Had shot my school mates dead.

Within a year, the robots ruled,
Humans were just trash,
Last in line, no room, no time,
Forgotten in a flash.

Then they went and killed the guy,
Who charged them up at night,
They all went flat, well fancy that,
No robots left to fight.

The Lockdown Poems

Home

Home is where the heart is,
And where we all must stay.
However hard this sounds to you,
Look on it this way.

The sun has started shining,
We see the flowers grow,
The mornings seem much brighter,
And warmer winds now blow.

As Spring replaces Winter,
And day defeats the night,
The Earth will keep revolving,
And the World will be alright.

March 24th 2020
Written as the UK went into national lockdown

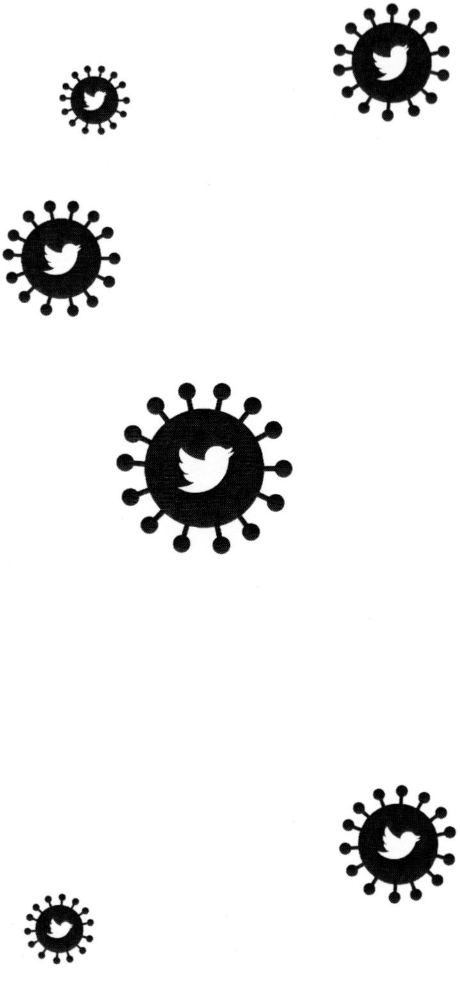

The Real Virus

To wish someone dead
is a terrible thing,
humanity trashed in a post.
To tweet out such views,
in response to the news,
is the virus we should fear the most.

This anger that boils
in the hearts of our race,
is born from injustice and fear.
To heal this we must
work together in trust,
Humanity could disappear.

The anti-biotic
we urgently seek
is collectively working as one,
with a willingness to
consider each view
and be kinder when all this is done.

April 7th 2020
When we woke up to the news that the PM had caught the Covid virus.

The Dandy Lion

Roaring round the garden,
Dressed in his Sunday best,
Popping up in lovely lawns,
And spreading out when pressed.

A splash of yellow sunshine,
Wildly roaming free,
A diuretic detox, for a
Sweeter garden pee !

Time-telling childhood blow-balls,
Torpedo on a stem,
Nice with ice and burdock,
(That refreshing little gem).

A mascot for the army,
Resilient and strong.
A source of golden nectar,
For the bees all summer long.

A weedy lion for the quacks,
To take all pains away,
But most of all, a sign that it's a
Blue sky sort of day.

April 26th 2020
When lockdown led me to discover the garden.

My Secret Garden

In my dreams I have a garden,
Filled with scented flowers
With fountains and a waterfall,
Where I can sit for hours.

Sunny glades and grottos
That inspire me every day,
A beautiful enormous lawn,
Where children come and play.

Yet sadly, this is just a dream,
No garden do I own,
My home is in a block of flats,
I live here all alone.

But then I had this cunning plan,
And please, I ask, don't laugh,
I've built my own small garden,
In the bathroom, in my bath.

I ordered in the compost,
And filled it to the brim
Then planted four geraniums,
And popped a palm tree in.

I added water features,
By connecting up the taps,
Into a kitchen colander,
With pebbles in the gaps.

I've left the plug hole open,
So the water drains away,
And used the shower fixture,
So it rains a bit each day.

And Oh, I cannot tell you,
What a picture! What a view,
There's nothing else quite like it,
When I'm sitting on the loo.

April 29th 2020
When we all longed for green space and I started to appreciate that not everyone had outdoor space they could escape into.

The Big One Hundred

Ground control to Captain Tom,
I hope you've got your glasses on.
What you've done is just amazing,
And so very profile raising,
Yorkshire's latest greatest favourite son.

Ground control to Colonel Tom,
A hundred years, and now your number one!
You'll never walk alone,
Through the courage that you've shown,
We're so inspired, by what you've gone and done.

Happy 100th Birthday Sir!

April 30th 2020
A new national hero was discovered in Yorkshire and the nation celebrated his 100th birthday.

Furlough

Locked down, locked in.

Taking it nervously, on the chin.

Home, whilst others work so hard,

Feeling guilty in my yard.

Who am I, I ask myself,

Left isolated on the shelf?

Keeping busy every day,

Yet worries do not go away.

Suddenly, or so it seems,

I'm not needed in the teams.

I know I shouldn't feel this way,

When others have to work all day.

But honestly, nowhere to go,

My life is now one long furlooooooooooo.

May 9th 2020
We learnt a new word to describe how many of us spent our days,
The National Furlough left many feeling isolated from work and colleagues.

The Lanes

You just can't beat a country lane,
Especially in the sun,
The perfect place to stretch your legs
Or set off for a run.

"You never know what's waiting,
round the corner", people say,
Then a stunning view appears on cue,
And takes your breath away.

The hedgerows full of busy bees,
And blue forget-me-nots!
Whilst benches found along the way
Make perfect picnic spots.

A flock of lambs are playing,
In fields along the hedge,
Beyond stone walls, where nature crawls,
Up to the tarmac edge.

Divert down dusty foot paths,
Clamber over stiles,
Meet dead ends, round muddy bends,
And walk those extra miles.

Encounter long lost villages,
And country house estates,
Admire those pretty gardens,
And the colour of their gates.

The Lanes all lead to somewhere,
And nowhere far away,
In truth, just round the corner,
You can lose yourself all day.

May 15th 2020
As lockdown continued, we were allowed to go out for a walk once every day. The nearby countryside became our faraway escape.

Missing in Action

I stopped sending you presents when I got no thanks,
Stopped writing you letters when I got back blanks,
Yes I've made my mistakes, but how my heart aches,
Just to hear a hello from you.

I stopped hoping to hear how you got on each year,
Stopped wishing you'd call, there were no calls at all,
I was told that you said you don't care if I'm dead,
But how my heart aches
Just to put both arms around you.

I stopped breathing last night, just a second, in fright,
I stopped thinking that you will be coming home too.
No I can't turn back clocks to see what that unlocks,
But how my heart aches,
Just to forget how much I miss you.

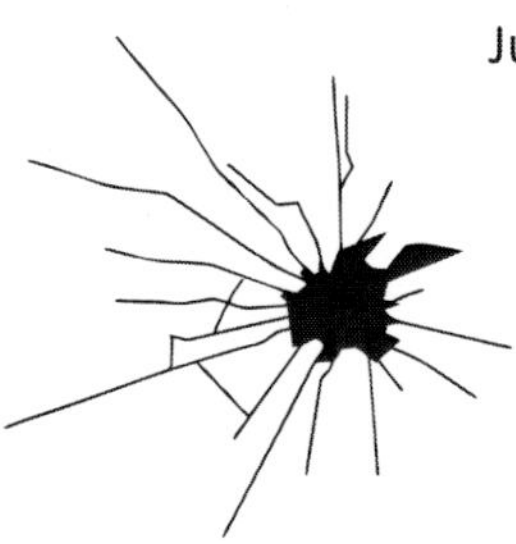

May 16th 2020
Families and friends were not allowed to meet, long distance relationships became strained. Old ghosts returned to haunt me.

Herd Mentality

"Two wrongs, they do not make a right!"
My grandma used to say,
I think that this is good advice
For all of us today.

Just because there's someone else,
Out there breaking rules,
Doesn't mean it's safer
For us all to act like fools.

Let's not act like lemmings,
Who just follow everyone,
But show some social common sense
And switch our brains back on.

May 31st 2020
As we were gradually released from lockdown, strict social distancing protocols were introduced. Not everyone felt the rules applied to them, including one or two high profile members of society.

I Should Be

I should be on my holidays,
I should be by the sea.
I should be out sunbathing,
That's where I now should be.

I should be choosing where to eat
As the sun goes down,
I should be putting on my shoes,
And heading into town.

I should be dancing on the beach,
With sangria in hand,
Then going for an evening swim,
And listening to a band.

I should be doing all these things,
I should be, so should you!
Instead we're grounded here at home,
Deciding what to do.

I could be putting up that shelf,
Or learning something new,
I could be in the garden, as there's
So much there to do.

Instead, I'm on the ipad,
And I'm checking on the flights,
For when all this is over,
We're away for 14 nights.

June 1st 2020
So many plans had to be put on hold, including the early summer holiday that many of us had taken for granted.

The Potting Shed Poet

You can't please all the plants all of the time,
Some need water, some are doing fine
It's complicated, keeping up the feeds,
Dead heading roses, pulling out the weeds.

There's always something on the list to do,
Fix one problem, then you find a few!
That laurel hedge is looking rather rough,
Too much water? Maybe not enough?

Other people's gardens look so neat,
Lush green lawns, and flower beds complete,
Mine is work in progress, I concede,
But all great gardens start off with a seed.

Gardening! If only I had known,
My poor green fingers worn down to the bone,
But then again, you reap just what you sow
And Great Oak trees from little acorns grow.

June 4th 2020
With millions of people forced to stay home, unable to go on holiday, many people rediscovered their gardens, tuned into "Gardeners World" and starting to grow with Monty Don.

Garden Party Invitation

We're having a party!
Here are the plans,
Please bring a towel
For washing your hands.

We will be outside,
But you can use the loo,
Just don't touch the woodwork,
Or door handles too.

No hugging or kissing,
You're not in my bubble,
But if you get desperate,
There's cushions to cuddle.

We'll sit well apart,
I don't mean to be rude,
But it's probably safer,
To bring your own food.

Typical, isn't it?
Sunshine for weeks,
But now we can meet up,
It's raining in sheets.

Still, this is progress,
And I'm longing to see,
My nearest and dearest
Up close in 3D.

June 17th 2020
The lockdown restrictions had eased, and we could meet up with our friends in the garden - but only if it stopped raining.

The Soller Train

On the Island of Mallorca,
There's this perfect little train,
That takes you out of Palma,
And then brings you back again.

Through the Tramuntana mountains,
To the famous Soller bay,
It's a marvellous adventure,
For an hour or so each way.

Those polished shiny carriages,
Attracting admiration,
From the tourists as they take a seat,
For their perambulation.

And then we're off through Palma's streets,
Trundling past the cars,
Waving at the locals,
Outside the Tapas bars.

At first it's rather urban,
Passing factories and yards,
There's little indication of the
Wonders on the cards.

But as we pass the picnic grounds,
The landscape starts to change,
Almond trees and a fresher breeze,
Blows down the mountain range.

In the village of Bunyola,
The train slows to a stop,
For here, a hundred years ago,
They'd load their market crop.

Then we're into darkness,
As a tunnel greets the train,
Black as night, then approaching light,
Then sunshine once again.

We stop again, just for the view,
High above the bay,
The driver has a cigarette,
And then we're on our way.

Now the train is getting faster,
Rolling down the mountain side,
We switchback in a tunnel,
Like a rollercoaster ride.

Past the backs of houses,
With their orange groves and vines,
And down into the station,
Past the locomotion lines.

So now the journey's over,
But our memories remain,
Of clear blue skies and mountain highs,
Onboard this little train.

And one day soon, I promise you,
We'll board an aeroplane,
Then come back to Mallorca,
And we'll do this all again.

June 19th 2020
The sunshine is great, but we long for escape from the lockdown world.

A Tale of Midsummer

Midsummer's Eve,
in the strangest of years.
When nightmarish creatures
became our worst fears.

Threatened by demons,
who flew through the air,
locked in our towers
and filled with despair

We trusted our kingdom
to do the right thing,
but nervously worried
of what that might bring.

We missed all the magic
of friends in hard times,
when sharing a hug became
one of life's crimes.

We clapped for the Carers,
our own fairy folk,
whilst damming the asses,
who thought it a joke.

Gargoyles and pixies were
flouting the rules,
as darkness descended
on all of our schools.

What a tale we will tell,
on next Midsummer's Eve,
of this time in our lives
we can hardly believe.

June 21st 2020
Midsummers eve in the strangest of years.

The New Normal

One metre plus,
Plus what? You may ask,
Well, extra hand washing,
And wearing your mask.

Three feet in old money,
Plus two or three inches,
So tighten your mask
Round your nose till it pinches.

These big plastic screens,
Are become the norm.
When off to the pub,
Go online for a form!

Whilst outside looks fine
For your own entertaining,
You best stay at home
If it looks like it's raining.

Don't face any strangers,
Their droplets may travel,
So keep at right angles,
As guidelines unravel.

And don't burst your bubbles,
This spreading must stop!
Six mates is best,
Or your bubble may pop.

At first we all thought,
This would soon go away,
But it looks like 'new normal'
Is now here to stay.

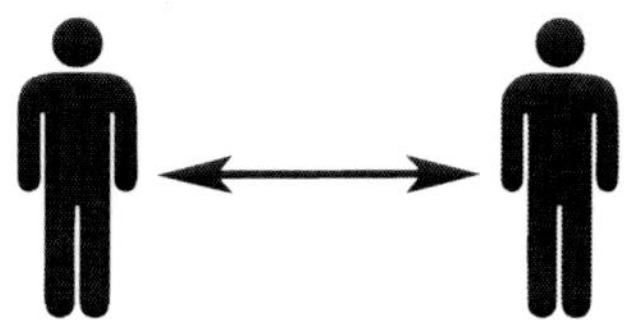

June 29th 2020
As we emerged from lockdown new rules for social distancing came into effect. Welcome to the new normal.

Back to Work Day

My last day on furlough,
So, with trepidation,
I pack my computer,
Then head for the station.

These one hundred days
At home, in the garden,
With chocolate and wine,
As my arteries harden.

Mixed feelings have I
Of this time spent at home,
My journeys restricted,
To dreaming alone.

Back in the real world,
Where all things will change,
I nervously view this,
As frighteningly strange.

We must all move forward,
I'm forced to admit,
But I rather liked furlough,
At least, most of it.

July 3rd 2020
As offices and factories started to open back up we said goodbye to our furloughs and headed back to work.

The Path

The heavy weight of deep regret,
That grows around the soul,
Slowing footsteps, bending backs,
Don't let it take control.

Of course, we'd do things differently,
If we could turn back time,
But living in the past, my friend,
Can be a bigger crime.

Our lives, they are not perfect,
So learn from past mistakes,
Now turn to face the future,
And embrace the path it takes.

August 29th 2020
Following a month or so of writers block I did my best to shake myself back into action.

My Happy Place

I'm happy in my garden,
A safe and happy place,
Where nature and my own bare hands,
Have learnt to interface.
I often let the plants dictate,
But gently nudge them on,
And help the flowers find their place,
To face the warming sun.
Some plants are welcome neighbours,
Blooming best in groups,
Whilst others thrive when on their own,
Away from other troops.
Weeds are not a problem,
If you spot them early on,
Stay diligent, and focus in,
Then pull up every one!

When the future seems to stumble,
Unsure of where it's going,
Great comfort can be found outside,
Just watching flowers growing.

September 9th 2020
The work carried out in the garden during the lockdown pays me back with a spectacular late Summer display.

Blinking Facemasks

Excuse me, but I have to ask,
Are you smiling beneath your mask?
It's hard to tell just what you're thinking,
So how about we smile by blinking?

A little blink plus a raised eyebrow,
Means "hello mate how are you now?"
A longer blink or maybe two,
Could mean "I have missed seeing you".

Three short blinks, and a little bow,
Gives a courteous smile that's quite highbrow.
But don't mix up a happy blink,
With a furtive cheeky wink.

For winking at a complete stranger,
Could generate some blinking danger!

September 18th 2020
Who would have thought that we'd get so used to wearing facemasks?

Blanket Coverage

A rhyme is like a comfort blanket,
Safe and soft and warm,
Wrapped around you like a dream,
Whilst verses slowly form.

A way back into childhood,
When lives were less involved,
When everything fell into place,
And cadences resolved.

In our complicated lives,
We need to find some time,
To snuggle up in poetry,
And lie back in a rhyme.

October 14th 2020
I was thinking about why I liked rhyming verse so much, and came up with this little rhyme whilst driving through the Peak District today.

20:20 Vision

I think we can see clearly now,
With 20:20 vision,
This year did not shape up too well,
Our progress hit remission.

Virus! Economic strain!
It's been a real stinker,
And makes you wonder what comes next,
Heading into winter.

Still, there were some positives,
We recognised the truth,
The NHS is brilliant,
And we're the living proof!

To all those medics saving lives.
The doctors, carers, nurses;
I'd like to send my heartfelt thanks,
Within these rhyming verses.

October 20th 2020
As the pandemic started to reveal a second wave, I thought about the medical staff who had been hard at it all year.

The Halloween Poems

The White Lady

Once upon a winter's night,
Under moonlit cover,
A local lass climbed Masson Hill,
To meet her secret lover.

They planned to meet upon the tower,
Then run away that night,
But as she reached the colder heights,
The frost began to bite.

She waited, as the snowflakes fell,
Where could her lover be?
Well, he was in the tavern,
With a tankard on his knee.

Whilst she was freezing on the hill,
He drank and fell asleep,
The snow became a blizzard,
Drifting round the tower deep.

Next morning, as the man awoke,
His memory returned,
He dashed off through the snow drifts,
Now worried, now concerned.

But as he reached the tower top,
He saw a dreadful sight,
His lover standing deathly still,
Had frozen overnight.

And now each year, At Halloween,
If snow falls on this hill,
You may just see her on this tower,
Waiting for him still.

Tommy's Last Climb

When battles rage across our land,
All men must soldiers be,
Prepared to fight for our beliefs,
For monarch and country.

And so it was in World War One,
When soldiers stationed near,
Kept their ammunition,
In the caves and caverns here.

One wet and stormy Halloween,
Young Soldier Tommy Stout,
Set out to climb this muddy slope,
And carry orders out.

Climbing up the steepest bank,
Towards where you stand now,
Instructed to bring bullets back
Despite the storm somehow.

Tommy knew he must succeed,
He'd almost reached the top,
When a flash of sudden lightening,
Brought the soldier to a stop.

The lightening split a nearby tree,
Which crashed onto the ground,
And rolled towards the soldier,
Causing mud to swirl around.

Poor Tommy didn't stand a chance,
Flattened by the tree,
Leaving just his rifle on the slope,
For all to see.

Though many came to find him,
His body was not found,
So somewhere, deep within the mud,
He's still here underground.

Rumbling Roop

Rumbling Roop was a miner,
He worked in the lead mines right here,
From the age of 6 to 35,
He dug in these caverns each year.

Poor Roop wasn't paid that much money,
A couple of pennies, or so,
But he loved working here with his brothers,
And loved eating food don't you know?

His mum was a cook up at Chatsworth,
She pinched a few cakes every week,
Then popped them in Roops' little snap tin,
To eat in the mines on his break.

By the time of his 35th birthday,
Roop was a quite portly chap,
Fatter than all t'other miners,
Chubby, beneath his flat cap.

His tummy would rumble like crazy,
So he ate even more every day,
His workmates said, "Roop's always eating,
He'll explode in the mines!" They would say.

Then one day, after his mother,
Stole a huge chocolate cake full of fudge,
Roop slipped and got stuck in the caverns,
Trapped there, he just couldn't budge,

They tried to use pulleys and donkeys,
To haul the poor lad safely free,
But Roop, well he just wasn't moving,
He's still there, between you and me.

The miners have long since departed,
Replaced by the tourists and show,
But sometimes, you still hear him rumble,
From deep in the shaft down below.

Naughty Ned

Naughty Ned, got out of bed
Late every single day,
He'd never listen to his Mum,
Or do a thing she'd say.

He kicked and screamed and shouted,
And then when he was done,
He terrorised his neighbours with his
slimy stink-bomb gun.

At school he was no better,
He bullied, punched and stole,
On-line he was even worse,
A rotten nasty troll.

"You will come to a sticky end"
His grandma said one day,
But Naughty Ned thought better,
And he always got his way.

On his sister's birthday,
He put cat food in her bed,
And smashed up all her presents,
Then he locked her in the shed.

The family planned a nice day out,
They'd go to Matlock Bath,
But Ned had plans to ruin it,
And went on the war path.

He pushed past all the children,
On the giant playground slide,
Knocking parents over,
As he rushed to take his ride.

Little girls were crying,
As he punched, and shoved and swore,
He was going on that slide,
At least ten times or more.

But parents watched in disbelief,
As Ned slid down the slide,
The ground below just opened up
and swallowed him inside.

The Matlock Lynx

Once upon some years ago,
A Zoo! On yonder hill,
Full of wild exotics,
And a famous Lynx, until...

This Wild Cat escaped one night,
And terrorised the town,
Eating all the farmer's sheep,
And deer owned by the crown.

A local group of village folk,
With pitchforks, nets and sticks,
Set out to catch the Wild Cat,
And stop its wicked tricks.

On Masson Hill, under the moon,
They waited for the beast,
To drag it back up to the Zoo,
So he could be released.

A brave and strong young fellow,
By the name of Billy Peck,
Jumped upon the creature,
But it turned and bit his neck.

Young Bill was carried down the slope,
But late next afternoon,
There was a transformation,
At the rising of the moon.

Thick hairs grew upon his hands,
Lynx ears on his head,
He howled and bent his arching back,
His eyes turned fiery red.

His teeth grew long and pointed,
Nails turned into claws,
He jumped out of the window,
And raced off on the moors.

The Wild Cat was never caught,
And Billy never found,
So take care here at Halloween,
In case they're both around.

The Creature on the Moors

"Don't go on the moors tonight,
beneath that cold moonlight.
Stay safe indoors, not on the moors,
please don't go out tonight".

He seemed a jolly fellow,
so I took his words in jest,
I hadn't thought of going out,
just staying with the rest.

But after listening to his words,
I seemed to want to go,
to take a stroll out on the moors,
a sort of dare, you know.

I slipped out of the pub back door,
and down the country lane,
across a style, for half a mile,
as it began to rain.

But as I passed a clump of trees,
a shadow caught my eye,
did I just see something move
against the evening sky?

A cold and prickly feeling,
started creeping up my spine,
I felt that I was being watched,
perhaps for quite some time.

Of course, I'd heard the stories,
of the creature on the moors,
but hadn't really thought it real,
just crazy old folklores.

A snap behind me made me jump,
and quickly spin around,
prepared to face a vampire,
or a ghoulish demon hound.

I fled back up the country lane,
and bolted through the door,
the landlord turned to speak to me,
"Have you been on t'moor?"

"Don't go on the moors tonight,
stay here, for in these parts,
after nine, it's free house wine,
and everyone plays darts".

Shine a Light

Today we're outside fixing bulbs,
To shine at Christmas time,
I'm looking closely at next doors,
But getting on with mine.

I like to put on quite a show,
But keep it neat and chic,
I start on Advent Sunday,
And it takes about a week.

I don't go in for reindeers,
Or snowmen on the roof,
Just garden lighting with a bit
Of sparkle in all truth.

Bring some light into the world,
To chase the dark away.
And twinkle like a Christmas star,
For Santa's on his way.

The Fall (Part one)

Dancing in the air waves,

Turning to the light,

The leaf twitched in the morning breeze,

Will he fall tonight?

In Spring, he grew with vigour,

Confident, but green,

Keen to reach his salad years,

But keener to be seen.

Throughout the long hot summer,

He stretched out in the sun,

Bending with prevailing winds,

And having lots of fun.

Yet now, so brown and brittle,

As Autumn breezes in,

He feels like he will crumble,

And he's looking thin.

Winter wraps its heavy coat,

Around the cooler sun,

Then snow falls on the countryside,

But leaf is clinging on.

Dancing in the air waves,

Turning from the light,

The leaf twitched in the cold night air,

Will he fall tonight?

The Rise (Part two)

Leaf trembled in the icy blast,
Twisting wildly round,
The only leaf left on the tree,
The others, on the ground.

He'd lived though all four seasons,
But knew his time had come,
The wind would surely take him,
And compost he'd become.

Then howling wind swept from the east,
And **SNAP** he felt it go,
Suddenly he's floating,
Caught in wind and snow.

High he flies, the tiny leaf,
Spinning round and round
Swirling past a steeple,
And down across the ground.

Round and round the roundabout,
Then over a street light,
Like a crazy fairground ride,
That goes on through the night.

He swirled into a market square,
Then swooped beneath a gate
And stopped outside the smart back door,
Of Church lane, number 8

"Look this one is perfect!"
Cried the giant looking down,
She picked him up, "this one is just,
The perfect shade of brown".

So now, leaf shines there proudly,
In a front-door Christmas wreath,
All golden, and with glitter on,
And two big balls beneath.

Christmas Wrap

The Christmas Elf was feeling down,
His spirit had been crushed.
Last to pack his presents up,
He felt that he had rushed.

Santa always told them,
"Take care when wrapping gifts!"
Good Elves wrap throughout the year,
And work in double shifts.

But not this Elf, oh no, not he,
He always left it late,
Then rushed around on Christmas Eve,
In such a flustered state.

As midnight struck he wrapped a book,
And then another one,
His pile had almost reached the roof,
Five minutes he'd be done.

Dashing down the corridor,
Towards the waiting sleigh,
Down the curly whirly slide,
On to the loading bay.

"Where HAVE you been?" said Santa,
"I'm sorry" said the Elf.
He gave Santa his presents,
And retreated to his shelf.

Santa smiled and said out loud,
"Well, better late than never,
Your wrapping has improved this year,
The little bows are clever!"

The little Elf puffed up with pride,
And wiped away a tear,
But secretly thought to himself,
"I'm safe until next year".

A Christmas Care

"We cannot use the sleigh you say?"
Said dumbstruck Santa Claus,
The sleigh was grounded, deemed unsafe,
By elf and safety laws.

The snow runners were buckled,
And made an awkward hissing,
Frost had rusted up the rails,
And Rudolf's nose was missing.

Throughout the summer season,
The work had not been done,
Forgotten, left alone to rust,
Ignored by everyone.

Call the Elf mechanics!
Find that reindeer nose,
Santa needs his sleigh tonight,
To travel through the snows.

Hauled into the garage,
So sleigh repairs could start,
Metal fixed and bolts were tested,
Bits were pulled apart.

"I think I've found the problem",
Claimed an Elf under the sleigh,
"Someone's turned the Care Switch off,
So Hope has gone away".

Without a Care we're finished,
Without a Hope we're lost,
A caring warming heart will always
Melt away the frost.

Well Santa's sleigh was sorted,
They flicked the switch back on,
And all the children got their gifts,
So joy to everyone!

The message in this story,
Is *"caring lights our way"*,
And isn't just for Christmas,
But a gift for every day.

Boxing Day Blues

I've got those Boxing Day Blues,
Whilst my stomach reviews,
All the food that I ate yesterday.
Did I really choose,
Such a vast range of booze?
My kidneys are melting away.

That one day of mirth,
Increases my girth,
Oh the food that now sits on my hips,
I'll hope for rebirth,
and increased self-worth,
With a diet of gym memberships.

Snooze-ology

I've found, as I get older,
An "ology" I love,
The art of having forty winks,
Or fifty, or above.

It's something I've perfected,
To get me through the day,
I simply have to close my eyes,
And soon I'm well away.

A little snooze each afternoon,
Restores my power cell,
But sometimes I just can't wake up,
And sleep all night as well.

The Resolution

New Year, New You,
is what they say.
A chance to start anew,
making huge improvements
is what I plan to do.

There's drinking lots more water,
going to a gym,
eating balanced food groups,
and hydrating the skin.

Watching where the money goes,
and putting some away,
then building up the savings
for a future rainy day.

There's trying to be nicer
to folk who drive me mad,
and being optimistic
when things are looking bad.

Also I will volunteer,
for something that's worthwhile,
and separate my plastics
to go that extra mile.

Wow, that reads like quite a list,
I'm filling up with doubt,
I didn't think I was that bad,
but now I'm freaking out.

I'll start with drinking water,
to get me into gear,
then look at all the other tasks
This time again next year.

Like Me

'Like me', go on 'like me' now,
I need to have those thumbs,
I log on 50 times a day,
Talking to my chums.

Befriend me, go on click me now,
Or send a social wave,
I won't be pushy, or intrude,
I promise to behave.

I need to up engagement,
To find my place on stage,
So go on, be a sport my friend,
Please just like my page.

What if we run out of likes?
No more to be found,
We'll have to switch the smart phone off,
And ask some mates around.

Thank You for reading my poetry seedlings.
I hope you enjoyed them.

You can read more rhymes on my website and Facebook page.

www.davidspoems.co.uk
www.facebook.com/davidspoems